The Tale of Castle Willow Tree

S-M.D.Petal

https://smdpetal.com

978-1-80541-518-3 (paperback)
978-1-80541-519-0 (hardcover)
978-1-80541-517-6 (ebook)

Once upon a time in a mystical forest, over an old cobblestone bridge, lived a beautiful Queen with bright pink chest-length hair, tropical ocean-blue eyes, elegant rich forest-green wings, milky pale skin and large pointy pixie ears. Elva was her name, but you see, Elva was no ordinary Queen – she was the Queen of the pixies.

Elva had a pet dragon named Drogo. Drogo was a sapphire-blue dragon with little tiger-orange wings and oat-coloured spikes all over his back, head and tail. Drogo also had a tiger-orange triangle spike at the end of his tail, sunflower-yellow horns, olive-green eyes, a big shiny smile, little legs and a cute baby pink nose. Sadly, Drogo, the Ocean dragon, was thought to be the last of his breed.

Elva had a daughter, Trixie. Trixie was a beautiful pixie with lime-green shoulder-length hair, arctic-blue elegant wings, and the same tropical ocean-blue eyes, large pointy ears and milky pale skin as her mum.

Elva, Trixie and Drogo were the protectors of the forest land, lakes, trees, plants, animals and other pixies.

As Elva's Kingdom was rising and thriving, there was a Dark Power lurking in the deepest left corner of the forest, building a plan to destroy Elva's Kingdom and its forest. However, the trees were always listening so, hearing of this plan, they passed along the information to the oldest tree, Orion.

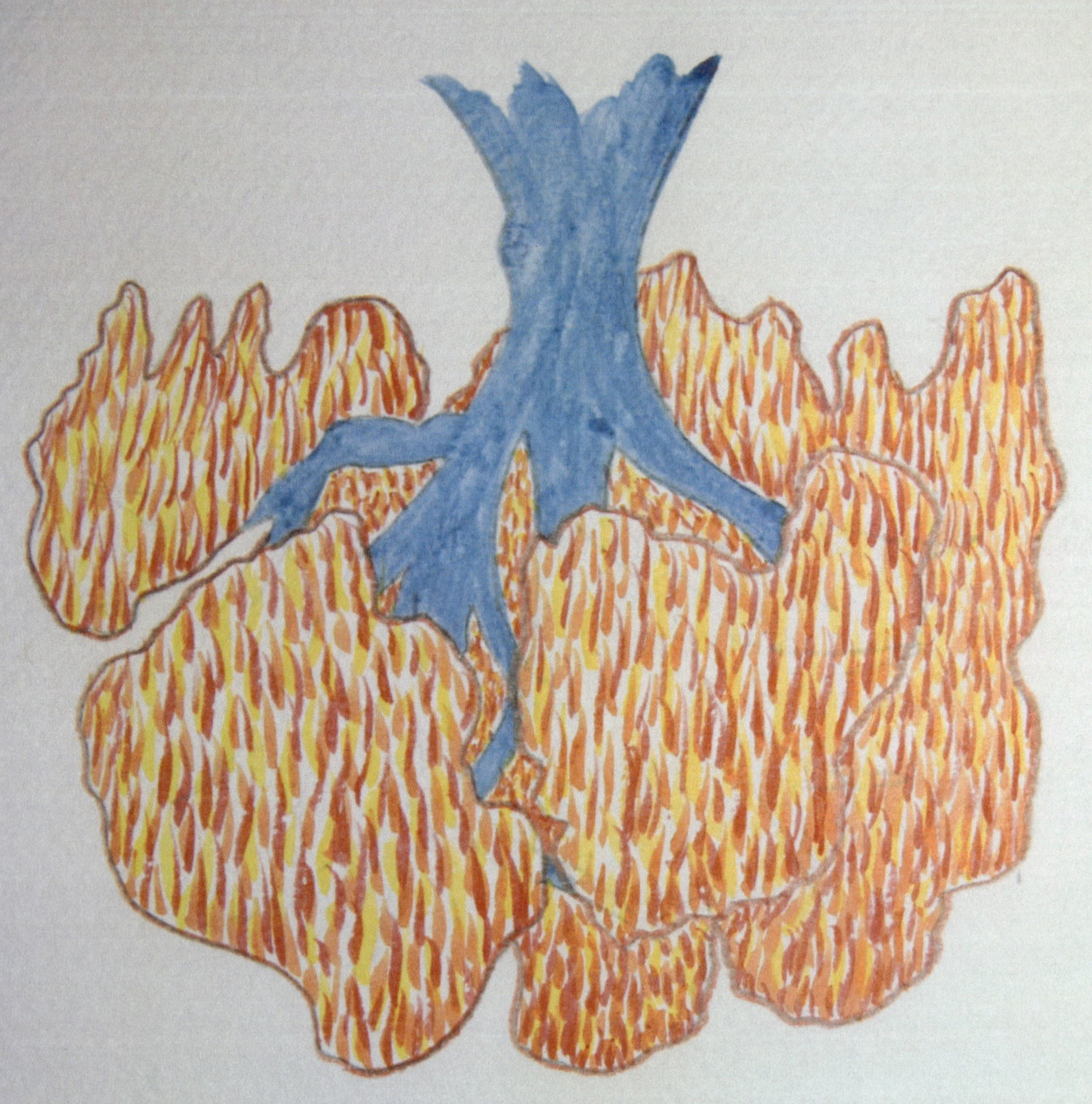

Orion was an extremely large tree with red, yellow and orange leaves, and he had a navy-blue trunk which meant Orion was the King of the Trees; all the other trees had purple, white and beige leaves with a pale pink trunk.

Drogo and Orion were out for a walk when they heard news of the Dark Power's plan. On receiving the information, Orion immediately told Drogo and sent him to tell Elva and Trixie what was happening.

Drogo flapped his little wings as fast as he could to reach Elva and Trixie. Elva told all the pixies in the Kingdom to gather in the famous courtyard of the castle at noon, where they made a simple plan to defeat the Dark Power in the forest.

When all the pixies knew of Elva's plan, they left to gather all the pixie dust that their pixie dust bags could hold. Then all the pixies, Elva, Trixie, Drogo and Orion took off, with Orion and Drogo leading the way, to defeat the Dark Power.

When they arrived at the deepest left part of the forest, the Dark Power laughed and said, "HAHAHA! Elva, Queen of Castle Willow Tree and protector of land and all living things, you have no power over me and I will take you down, but I will leave the big blue tree with the red, yellow and orange leaves. I like that tree he is magnificent. However, I am going to have to take over your Kingdom. Sorry in advance!"

Suddenly, a massive black storm cloud appeared in front of the pixies. Orion quickly said, "Hurry, pixies, the pixie dust!" As fast as they could, they all scattered the pixie dust in a big circle around the dark stormy cloud. Orion started to chant:

"With golden powers and trees so fine, let this dark storm be entwined with winds so high, I call to come alive and banish this evil from my sight."

Thankfully, that worked, and the dark storm disappeared, so Elva declared that there would be a large feast in celebration.

At the feast, all the pixies were having a blast. Drogo ate all the parsnips, and Orion had a bit too much dust bomb, which is a pixie-dust drink, so Drogo was laughing at him and decided to help him back to where he should have been standing.

One hundred and twenty years passed. Castle Willow Tree was now ten thousand years old and still standing tall and strong.

There had been no trouble in the Kingdom since the Dark Power was defeated.

Drogo was out in the forest looking for more parsnips to eat when he came across a sweet dragon called Oceana. Oceana was dark blue with baby-blue spikes all over her head, back and tail.

So, he invited Oceana to dinner at the Castle. Whilst they were having dinner, the creeper plant was climbing up the castle and started suffocating Castle Willow Tree.

After a while, the creeper plant decided to leave the Kingdom and never return, but there was some damage to the Castle, so Elva sent pixies to the golden forest to find the giant green wolf, and thankfully, the wolf came to fix the Castle.

As he had cubs to look after, the wolf arrived as fast as the wind, and once the castle was fixed, he left at the same speed!

Ten weeks had passed since the wolf had fixed the Castle and the Kingdom was thriving once again, but unbeknown to all in the Kingdom, a bad grey bunny with blue ears and a big blue fluffy tail was planning to take the golden Willow Tree seed in three weeks' time during the annual Walk of the Pixie Dust. Drogo and Oceana would be left at the castle.

Another three weeks had passed, and it was the day of the Walk of the Pixie Dust. Drogo and Oceana had gone for a romantic fly in the forest to collect more parsnips, carrots and onions.

The bad grey bunny broke into the Kingdom, bounced across the cobblestones and through the large oak door into Castle Willow Tree's foyer, up the long, old windy staircase to the very top, where the golden Willow Tree seed is kept in an oakwood and glass display cabinet.

The bad bunny quickly snatched the seed and made his way out of the castle and through the forest as fast as he could. Suddenly, the trees cast a net made from their roots over the bunny and the golden Willow Tree seed bounced along the floor and Drogo caught it in his little paws. "How dare you steal the seed of the Willow Tree Kingdom!" Drogo said in an outraged voice. Drogo quickly handed the seed to Oceana who placed the seed gently back where it belonged.

Willow.
Dingo.
Blue Falls.
Ocean.
Mango.
Troso.
Oceana.

Fifteen months had passed, and Drogo and Oceana had fallen more in love and all the pixies had come back to a surprise. Drogo and Oceana had five babies – Mango, Ocean, Blue Falls, Dingo and Willow.

Later, the winter festival arrived at the castle. Trixie took her mum, Elva, to the bridge to tell her about the baby she was having and that she was going to call her Scarlett after her grandma. Elva was over the moon with happiness and joy. Baby Scarlett was arriving soon. They returned to the castle and danced and enjoyed some festive winter pixie food.

Soon, the time had passed and Scarlett was born.

To celebrate her birth, the pixies threw a big party to shower her with blessings.

So, Elva, Drogo, Oceana, Mango, Blue Falls, Ocean, Dingo, Willow, Trixie, Scarlett and all the pixies and trees in Willow Tree Kingdom lived in happiness for eternity.

The End

S-M.D. Petal ©